Dr JAY

PASTORS & PROPHETS

PROTOCOL FOR HEALTHY CHURCHES

PASTORS & PROPHETS

PROTOCOL FOR HEALTHY CHURCHES

C. PETER WAGNER, EDITOR

WAGNER
PUBLICATIONS

Pastors and Prophets
Copyright © 2000 by C. Peter Wagner
ISBN 1-58502-015-X

Published by
Wagner Publications
11005 N. Highway 83, Colorado Springs, Colorado 80921
www.wagnerpublications.org

Cover design by Hala Saad, Vision Communications, 711 Lowell Street, Dallas, Texas 75214, (214) 827-0620

Interior design by Rebecca Sytsema

Rights for publishing this book in other languages are contracted by Gospel Literature International (GLINT). GLINT also provides technical help for the adaptation, translation, and publishing of Bible study resources and books in scores of languages worldwide. For further information, contact GLINT, P.O. Box 4060, Ontario, CA 91761-1003, USA. You may also send e-mail to glintint@aol.com, or visit their web site at www.glint.org.

1 2 3 4 5 6 7 8 9   06 05 04 03 02 01 00

CONTENTS

CHAPTER ONE

PROPHETIC PROTOCOL

by C. Peter Wagner

The government of the church is finally taking its biblical shape!

According to Ephesians 4, when Jesus ascended to heaven, He left in place both the government and the operational system that He had designed for His body, the body of Christ. For two to three centuries the church followed Jesus' plan, and it worked! A major outcome was one of the most amazing phenomena of all recorded human history, namely the Christianization of the entire Roman Empire.

Then a surprising thing happened. Church leaders thought that they had better ideas for the government of the church, so they reengineered it. The net result is that for about 1600 years the church has operated with less than ideal government.

That unbiblical pattern is now changing before our very eyes. For the first time in centuries, the biblical government of the church is once again being recognized. The key text for this in Ephesians 4 is verse 11: "And [Jesus] Himself gave some to be apostles, some prophets, some evangelists, and some pastors and teachers." When these "big five" are in place, then all the saints will be equipped for ministry and the church will once again operate as it was originally designed to do (see Eph. 4:12).

Relationships

Let's say that church leaders have now come to recognize the gifts and offices constituting the "big five," which a rapidly increasing number of them actually do. An immediate challenge that arises from this is to come to an understanding of how each of these five offices properly relates to the other four. It could well turn out that the most difficult combination of all ten possibilities is how pastors are supposed to relate to prophets and how prophets are supposed to relate to pastors.

That is what this book is about.

In these first two chapters, I want to paint a broad picture with a historical context, and then make a practical application. The rest of the chapters are written by pastors who find themselves among a very select group—those local church pastors who have a public track record of establishing positive and productive relationships with prophets.

Two Ways of Ordering the "Big Five"

We can look at the order of the government offices of the church from either of two different perspectives, the *ecclesiastical* order and the *historical* order. It is important for us to understand them both.

Ecclesiastically, our starting point is Ephesians 2:20: "[The household of God] is built on the foundation of the apostles and prophets, Jesus Christ Himself being the chief cornerstone." No comment needed. This, however, is not the only Scripture that tells us that the order starts with apostles and prophets. The Bible also says, "And God has appointed these in the church: *first* apostles, *second* prophets, third teachers . . ." (1 Cor. 12:28). After apostles and prophets, then, would come teachers, as well as pastors and evangelists.

Understanding the exact place of evangelists may not be that crucial for us at the moment, since the primary function of evangelists is *outside* of the church, persuading unbelievers to become Christians. Consequently, that leaves pastors and teachers whose primary function is *inside* the church. While the two may be different in their giftings, it is important to recognize that many individuals in our churches today have dual gifts and offices. They are, at the same time, both pastors and teachers.

When we look at this *historically*, however, we discover that the order has been reversed, at least it began to be reversed after the first couple of centuries:

♦ **Teachers** have been in place through all of church history. There has never been a time when teachers have not been recognized.

♦ **Pastors** came into their own with the Protestant Reformation. Previously, the unbiblical office of "priest" had substituted for it.

♦ **Evangelists** were not widely recognized as such until Charles Finney arrived on the scene about 150 years ago. It will come as a surprise to many to learn that at that time there was a good bit of controversy as to whether or not it would be proper to recognize the office of evangelist. I'll come back to that in a moment.

Intercessors began to be accepted in the 1970s. I realize that intercessors are not named in Ephesians 4:11 as a governmental office, but I want to mention them because they do constitute a notable *catalytic* office that has played a vital role in opening the way for the last two.

♦ **Prophets** began gaining visibility in the 1980s. I do not mean to imply that there were no prophets before 1980, but rather that their more widespread recognition began at that time.

♦ **Apostles** started to take their rightful place in the government of the church in the 1990s. It is ironic that what should have been first *ecclesiastically*, namely apostles and prophets, have actually turned out to be last *historically*!

Today's Comfort Zones

Let's take a look at what the recognition of each of these offices did to our comfort zones when they first came to the attention of the wider body of Christ:

1. **Teachers.** Teachers have probably never been much of a threat to anyone. I first noticed this while watching professional football games on television. When the outcome of a certain game is no longer in question and a referee makes a close call that might have gone either way, the announcer frequently says that the decision was purely

"academic." I looked "academic" up in the dictionary and it says, "Theoretical or hypothetical; not practical or directly useful." Think of it. Who could possibly be threatened by a teacher?

2. **Pastors.** The role of pastor falls well within the comfort zone of the Protestant part of Christianity. In fact, ever since the sermon has taken its place as the central event in the weekly life of a typical congregation, pastors have been seen primarily as teachers.

3. **Evangelists.** The controversy surrounding Finney did, in fact, take many out of their comfort zones. Not all Christian leaders were ready to recognize that certain individuals merited being called "evangelists." For example, Lyman Beecher, a notable seminary president in his day, was particularly upset with Finney and Finney's so-called "new measures." In fact, Beecher wrote a rather nasty personal letter to Finney saying, "I know your plan and you know I do. You mean to come into Connecticut, and carry a streak of fire to Boston. But if you attempt it, as the Lord liveth, I'll meet you at the state line, and call out all the artillerymen, and fight every inch of the way to Boston, and I'll fight you there."[1]

This seems humorous to us today because recognizing certain individuals as "evangelists" is no longer a serious point of controversy. We are comfortable with it.

4. **Intercessors.** Intercessors are now generally accepted in our churches across denominational lines. It is not unusual to visit a church and be introduced to someone as "one of our intercessors." But it took 15 or 20 years for this to happen. This clearly was not the case back in 1970.

There is still somewhat of a residue of opposition to the office of intercessor, especially when it is related to prophetic intercession or strategic-level intercession, although the opposition is rapidly diminishing.

5. **Apostles.** Apostles are the latest of these offices to be recognized, and I must admit that I am surprised at the apparent low level of controversy over the last few years. I would have thought that the notion of contemporary apostles would have pulled people out of their comfort zones at least as much as evangelists did 150 years ago. But so far I haven't seen much of it. Perhaps it is a time bomb waiting to go off. Perhaps there are other reasons.

6. **Prophets.** I saved prophets for last because the idea of individuals who have the gift and office of prophet has been particularly difficult, and it has stretched the comfort zones of Christian leaders more than any of the others. Jesus actually prepared us for this when He took on some religious leaders of His day. He said, "Woe to you! For you build the tombs of the prophets, and your fathers killed them" (Luke 11:47).

With this in mind, let's focus on prophets for the time being.

Why Are Prophets So Upsetting?

If prophets are more upsetting than the other governmental offices in the church, why would this be the case? I think there are several reasons.

Old Covenant vs. New Covenant

First of all, we read more about prophets in the Bible than we do about any of the other four governmental gifts. Throughout the whole Old Testament, prophets were extremely active, and even then they weren't very popular. "They were stoned, they were sawn in two, were tempted, were slain with the sword. They wandered about in sheepskins and goatskins, being destitute, afflicted, tormented" (Heb. 11:37). The upshot of this is that, even today, our mental images and our stereotypes of what prophets are supposed to be come largely from the Old Testament.

As a result of this, many church leaders have not understood the differing roles of prophets under the Old Covenant as opposed to the New Covenant. This is the difference between law and grace. Admittedly, it is not easy to move into a grace mode with unpopular prophets.

No one has addressed this issue more clearly than Mike Bickle, the leader of the "Kansas City Prophets." He has been widely recognized as one of the most sought-after pastors of prophets in America. Here is how he explains the difference between New Testament prophets and Old Testament prophets:

"In the New Testament, instead of stoning prophets when they make mistakes, the leaders are instructed to 'let two or three prophets speak, and the others judge' (1 Cor. 14:29). The Revised Standard Version translates the passage: 'let the others weigh what is said.' Paul gives similar instructions to the church in Thessalonica: 'Do not quench the Spirit. Do not despise prophecies. Test all things; hold fast what is good' (1 Thes. 5:19-21).

"We [in Kansas City] don't stone people if they miss it

once; neither do we believe everything they say, whether they are accurate 51 percent or 99 percent of the time."

Bickle goes on to say, "This idea of prophetic people with subtle impressions of the Holy Spirit making mistakes some of the time is difficult for many conservative evangelicals. The reason, of course, is that they have failed to understand the transition in prophetic ministry. While they clearly see other aspects of the Old Testament changing under the New Covenant, their understanding of prophetic ministry is still based on an Old Testament model."[2]

Prophets will continue to be upsetting if we persist in evaluating apostles, evangelists, pastors, and teachers by New Covenant criteria, while evaluating prophets by Old Covenant criteria. A double standard won't work well.

Hearing Directly from God

A second reason why prophets are so upsetting is that they are in direct communication with God. It is true that every one of us should hear from God, but prophets, by their supernatural gifting, are supposed to do it the best. My definition of the gift of prophecy is: "The special ability that God gives to certain members of the Body of Christ to receive and communicate an immediate message of God to His people through a divinely anointed utterance."[3] The notion that certain individuals can hear more frequently and more accurately from God than other Christians continues to pull many out of their comfort zone. It causes two things to happen:

1. It upsets cessationists more than any other spiritual gift does. Dyed-in-the-wool cessationists believe that a whole list of spiritual gifts such as tongues and miracles and dis-

cernment of spirits and healings ceased with the close of the apostolic age and the completion of the New Testament canon. But prophecy is by far the most troublesome of all.

This was highlighted by the publication of Jack Deere's *Surprised by the Power of the Spirit* (Zondervan), which many regard as the theological coup de grâce of cessationism. In it, he tells of how he originally planned to do a chapter on prophecy, but when he started, he found that the subject was so crucial to his argument that he needed to do a whole new book, not just a chapter, on the subject. He did, and it is called *Surprised by the Voice of God* (Zondervan).

2. The idea of prophets hearing directly from God leads noncessationists, who agree that true prophets are ministering today, to impose higher standards of perfection on prophets than they would impose on teachers, pastors, evangelists, or apostles. This clearly sets the stage for potential trouble, especially when local church pastors have been programmed with this mentality.

Prophets Are Strange!

A third reason why prophets are upsetting to some has to do with their personalities. Although not all prophets would fit this stereotype, most Christian leaders who have moved in circles in which prophets are active would agree that many prophets are somewhat strange. They are messy. Sometimes they don't have good manners. Stephen Mansfield suggests some reasons for this in his chapter. This makes prophets unusual. To say the least, prophets are not average people.

Someone said that trying to get prophets together is like trying to herd cats!

Protocol Is Fuzzy

Fourth. The body of Christ lacks a spiritual protocol that would enable prophets to play by the rules. Not everyone agrees on the rules for prophetic ministry either in local churches or "translocally." This is as confusing as it would be to have some baseball teams which assume that three outs end an inning while others think they should be allowed four outs. No wonder that many prophets upset pastors and other church leaders—they haven't agreed on the rules before starting the game.

 In my opinion, this is one of the highest priority challenges facing the current New Apostolic Reformation. We must focus our energies on developing a spiritual protocol for prophets and prophetic ministries. This must be done so well that it is widely accepted among church leaders who believe in prophecy. We need to agree on the rule book, and we need to do it now. Tomorrow may be too late!

Notes

1. Sydney Ahlstrom, *A Religious History of the American People* (New Haven CT: Yale University Press, 1972), p. 461.
2. Mike Bickle, *Growing in the Prophetic* (Orlando FL: Creation House, 1996), p. 97.
3. C. Peter Wagner, *Your Spiritual Gifts Can Help Your Church Grow* (Ventura CA: Regal Books, 1979, 1994), p. 229.

CHAPTER TWO

TEAMING PROPHETS WITH PASTORS

by C. Peter Wagner

If, as I suggested in the last chapter, we need to develop a book of protocol for prophets and prophetic ministries, where do we start?

The Most Crucial Areas

Let's take another look at the "big five" governmental gifts of Ephesians 4:11, apostles, prophets, evangelists, pastors, and teachers, plus the catalytic gift of intercessor.

How prophets should relate to all other five in the list is a primary question. However, I have concluded that the two most crucial areas of them all for establishing prophetic protocol at the moment are:

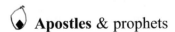 **Apostles** & prophets

◉ **Pastors** & prophets

I don't mean to imply that the other three are not important, because they are. I do have certain reasons, however, to
assign them a lower priority than apostles and teachers, at least
at the present time. Here are my reasons:

♦ **Teachers** have a broad overlap with pastors. It is true that
some pastors clearly are not teachers and that some teachers do not have an ounce of pastoral gifting. However, go
down the list of churches in your phone book and in most
cases you will find that a prominent part of the job description of the pastor, no matter what denomination, is to
teach the congregation through the Sunday sermon week
after week. Consequently, if we work out the protocol for
prophets and pastors, we are thereby including the majority of teachers.

♦ **Intercessors** have at least as broad an overlap with prophets as teachers have with pastors. Again, the overlap may
not be 100 percent. But whatever the percentage might
turn out to be, it is very high. This means that there would
not be a big difference between a rule book for *interces-
sory* protocol and a rule book for *prophetic* protocol.

♦ **Evangelists.** I must confess that I do not as yet have the
understanding that I wish I had on the gift and office of
evangelist. I have many books in my library on evangelism and evangelists, but I also have a lurking hunch that
in the near future God will be revealing exciting new in-
sights about evangelists that are not found in those books.
So I think that developing protocol between evangelists
and prophets is somewhere down the road. I'm happy to

put it on hold for now.

Apostles and Prophets

Before getting to the major theme of this book—how pastors relate to prophets—let me say a brief word about apostles and prophets. In my observation, the relationships between apostles and prophets have been coming along nicely as this book goes to press. By this I do not mean to imply that we have arrived. No. We have come a long way, but we still have a long way to go. Let's keep in mind that the process of working this out only began around 20 years ago. That means that our track record covers only one percent of Christian history. As a point of comparison, it took the church almost 10 times that long to decide which 27 books should be in the New Testament canon! It may not be far out of order, then, to appeal for a bit of patience and tolerance as we work through this process.

I am only one of many Christian leaders whom God has called in America and around the world to focus on these issues at the present time. One day we will be able to compile and analyze numbers of different reports. Meanwhile, however, here are four important developments that I see from my own perspective in facilitating relationships between apostles and prophets:

Paul-Silas Relationships

♦ Many apostles have developed a Paul-Silas relationship with prophets and they work together as a team. I think of Rice Broocks and Jim Laffoon of Morningstar as an example. Jim Hodges and Barbara Wentroble of the Federation of Ministers and Churches would be another.

My relationship to Chuck Pierce would also fit the description. There are many more.

♦ The Apostolic Council of Prophetic Elders held its first meeting in early 1999. This organization brings together 20-25 recognized prophets for peer-level interaction at least twice a year. I convene the meetings and I preside in my role as apostle of the group. This is specifically what I call a "horizontal apostolic" role, meaning that, outside of the meeting of that group itself, I do not exercise any "vertical" or ongoing apostolic "covering" over any of the individual prophets. This, by the way, is a very important distinction to keep in mind.

♦ The New Apostolic Roundtable is a similar group of peer-level apostles who meet on a regular basis for building relationships and mutual accountability. These apostles have agreed to bring with them to the meetings a selected number of prophets with whom they have developed a Paul-Silas relationship. Such interaction is contributing greatly to working out protocol between apostles and prophets.

♦ I have recently published a new book, *Apostles and Prophets* (Regal Books), which, to my knowledge, is the most detailed analysis of the protocol between apostles and prophets available to date. This book provides many details related to the three points above.

So much for apostles and prophets. Now, let's consider the question of how pastors and prophets productively relate to one another.

The *Ministries Today* Cover

Nothing could better highlight the current widespread misunderstandings between pastors and prophets than this cover from the May/June 2000 *Ministries Today*:[1]

Obviously, this is not a picture of every prophet. It does not pretend to be anything other than a stereotype. I hope that no one takes offense because I have chosen to use it. But I must say that, in my opinion, the artist, Gary Locke, deserves some kind of an award for his skill in portraying exactly how a surprising number of pastors see prophets today. Is this the way that prophets *ought* to be seen by pastors? Certainly not. But the question isn't really that important in light of the fact that this is actually the perception that many pastors *do* have of prophets in their midst.

Denial Won't Work!

I don't think that the best approach to this situation would be denial on the basis that no problem should exist. That would be sticking our head in the sand. It may be true that there *shouldn't* be any problem, but we cannot escape the fact that one surely does exist. In fact, the cover article inside the magazine carries the title "Pastors vs. Prophets." The operative word in that title is "versus." What we are facing is a perceived adversarial relationship between two of the Ephesians 4:11 "big five" governmental offices of the church.

Here is an example that, unfortunately, is not uncommon. A pastor from Alabama says, "My wife and I, as pastors, were involved in the prophetic movement but have now removed ourselves from this camp. We stepped away because we saw abuse of the prophetic. The personal power many of these prophets have over people is too hard to resist. They use their 'words' to gain position, control and notoriety among Christians. . . . We have confused monetary gain with maturity, we have confused charisma with charac-

ter, and we have confused performance with power."[2] This
pastor puts into words exactly what the *Ministries Today* art- ✓
ist draws into a cartoon.

We Must Overcome Quickly

This is a situation that must be overcome decisively and very
soon! Look at the picture again. Is the prophet happy? No!
Is the pastor happy? No! Are the people happy? No! In
fact, the pews are virtually empty! This is anything but a
healthy church.

I have no doubt that we are going to overcome the current
state of affairs. Soon after the *Ministries Today* came out I
called the editor, Larry Keefauver. I said, "Larry, when I
first saw the cover I was upset. I preferred to be in denial.
But reality soon set in, and now I want to congratulate you
for surfacing a vital issue that we must face head-on."

I told him that I wanted to be part of dealing with the
problem. Then I said, "Larry, it will take a while. But the
next time you have a pastor and a prophet on your cover, they
will have their arms around each other. Wait and see!" I
sincerely hope that this book will be one small step in the
direction that we want to head, and that it why I used the
subtitle: *Protocol for Healthy Churches.*

The Rest of the Book . . .

I am neither a pastor nor a prophet. I am an apostle and a
teacher (one of those teachers without the pastoral gift!). So
here is how we are going to proceed: I will conclude this
chapter by directing my words to pastors. Although I am not
a prophet, I have been commissioned as a spokesperson for

some well-known prophets through the Apostolic Council of Prophetic Elders. Following this, four respected pastors will contribute chapters. Each of these pastors has had positive experiences in relating to prophets, and you will feel their heart as you read. Therefore pastors who read this book will first *receive* a word about their relationship to prophets and secondly the pastors who write in this book will *give* a word about their relationship to prophets. To my knowledge, this book is a first of its kind.

A Word to Pastors

My career as a professor of church growth has given me more than an average love and appreciation for the ministry that God has entrusted to pastors. I am happiest when I can somehow add some value to a pastor and see that person become everything that God wants them to be. In order for this to happen as it should, 2 Chronicles 20:20 becomes an operative Scripture: "Believe in the Lord your God, and you shall be established; believe His prophets, and you will prosper."

My heart's desire is that every pastor who reads this book will prosper. In this I would include your relationship to God, your family, your health, your social life, your finances, and the congregation you are pastoring. Your pews should not be empty like the ones on the *Ministries Today* cover. They should be full and getting fuller week after week. One of the things that the Bible says will help make this happen is to believe God's prophets. Yet, in many cases you can't bring yourself to believe the prophets because they have wounded you at one time or another. Needless to say, this blockage to God's best for you must be removed.

I felt that I was partially to blame for some of this when, in

1999, I convened the first National School of the Prophets in Colorado Springs. Soon after that event word began to come back to me from pastors of churches whose members had attended and then gone back home and upset their churches. That was a shock to me! I immediately realized that we hadn't given the people enough instruction on how prophets, or would-be prophets, are supposed to relate to their pastors.

How to Intimidate a Pastor

I can imagine what happened in many cases. I can picture a church member in conversation with their pastor which goes something like this: "Pastor, I have just come back from the National School of the Prophets in Colorado Springs. It was awesome. What incredible worship with 2500 people praising the Lord together! And I heard the prophets talking about Y2K. If you were a good shepherd, you would be doing a lot more to protect your people from Y2K!"

This kind of thing does not make a pastor's day. Such a statement is designed to intimidate the pastor. If the pastor politely hums or haws or hesitates in agreeing with the church member, the next cannon ball is ready: "Pastor, do you know who I heard? Bill Hamon and Paul Cain and Cindy Jacobs and Mike Bickle and Rick Joyner and others like them. Do you think they could be wrong?"

Here is the issue: A church member is trying to require the pastor to move in light that the pastor has not received from God! I hate to say it, but this is nothing less than a spirit of manipulation and control in operation. It may not make the pastor's day, but it surely makes Satan's day! We should have warned the church member not to commit such an error of judgment.

Y2K Prophecies

The Y2K issue is a good case in point. Let's consider it. Looking back, we can now analyze Y2K objectively. First of all, not all the prophets who spoke in the National School of the Prophets expressed the same degree of concern about the approaching Y2K. I can remember that Paul Cain, for example, had very little worry. He said, "God is not so concerned about Y2K as He is about Y-O-U!" Others, however, sensed a considerable degree of danger for society and for the church. Before the conference the prophets all met together and agreed to issue a brief public statement that Y2K should be taken seriously and the statement was publicly read in the National School of the Prophets. It was intentionally worded to avoid excessive alarm. This was what our hypothetical church member would have taken back to the pastor.

Was our statement about Y2K right or wrong? If we think this question through, we will have important clues as to the protocol for pastors to relate to prophets.

The answer is that it was either right or wrong—depending on your perspective. To illustrate, here are two opinions expressed after everybody knew that January 1, 2000 did not turn out to be a catastrophe.

♦ One megachurch pastor, who will go unnamed, commented, "Many [prophets] were saying that Y2K was the end, or at least the beginning of the end. The word on the streets was that we needed to buy gold, get cash, store water and prepare to generate our own electricity. The most dominant Christian voices were encouraging us to pull our money out of a fragile stock market, and warning that free trade was weakening the United States."

Was this pastor wrong? Obviously not. It is an accurate statement of some things that were happening as we moved from one century to another.

♦ Another way of looking at it came over the Internet from secular scholar Dr. Ted Daniels whose work has been referenced in *New York Times, Newsweek, Boston Globe* and other publications. Daniels says: "Whatever else it may have been, Y2K was one of the most successful prophecies on record. It seems on cursory examination that since nothing much happened, the Y2K prophecies failed. But this assessment of the situation misses the real nature of prophecy, in which prediction plays only a secondary role.

"Noah is the model of prophetic failure. Yes, things turned out exactly as he predicted, but the point was that people were supposed to listen and change their behavior, forestalling the dreaded outcome. Noah failed in his mission, while the Y2K prophets succeeded in theirs. They urged us to change our ways and spend untold billions on consultants and software. We spent, like good capitalist believers knowing the real route to kingdom outcome, and we are saved . . ."³

Prophecy Is Conditional

Whether you agree with Daniels or not, he nevertheless brings up a very important dimension of prophecy, namely that most prophecy is conditional. The Bible is clear that changed behavior can often change God's declaration. The conversion of Nineveh is an outstanding biblical example.

But another crucial factor enters the process, namely intercession. Targeted intercession, empowered by the Holy

Spirit, can move the hand of God in another direction. Prophecy often is a warning of what will happen if the people of God do not stand in the gap. This could well have been the case with Y2K. I know that some will say that this way of looking at it can be a "cop out." This is a valid comment, and the fact of the matter is that no one could absolutely prove it either way.

The point I am making is not directly related to Y2K, but I am using Y2K as an example of the kind of consideration that needs to guide us as we develop protocol between pastors and prophets.

In a recent meeting, the Apostolic Council of Prophetic Elders had a long discussion on improvements needed among prophets to help avoid the situation depicted on the *Ministries Today* cover. They were grieved that some who attend our conferences would return to their churches and violate the authority of pastors. They were grieved that some prophets would prophesy judgment with no tears and compassion. They were grieved that some too readily use the expression "Thus saith the Lord," when milder expressions could just as well be used. They were grieved over occasional lack of discernment in proclaiming revelation that should have been kept to themselves.

Teaming Prophets with Pastors

Pastors need prophets. Their churches will be healthier with them than without them. Prophets, along with apostles, are the foundation of the church. But they must understand how they can relate effectively to each other.

A starting point must be recognizing that the pastor is the spiritual authority over the local church. Anything that upsets this pastoral role is not the will of God in a healthy church. In the local church, a prophet is a member of the team, but not the team's leader. This is strongly highlighted in the following chapters.

I like to think of pastors and prophets as pitchers and catchers. When you watch a baseball game on television, the camera is on the pitchers and catchers the majority of the time. They are not the whole team, but they definitely are the core of the defense. Notice that the pitcher is the authority. The pitcher is the only player who is credited with the win or charged with the loss of the game. In a local church, the pastor is the pitcher and the catcher is the prophet.

The catcher gives the signals to the pitcher. But every signal is subject to the final authority of the pitcher. In the great majority of the cases, the pitcher accepts the signals from the catcher and throws accordingly. But sometimes no. The catcher advises the pitcher, but is also subject to the final authority of the pitcher. Over the years, this baseball protocol has been well developed.

Protocol for Pastors and Prophets

Here is how I think that the pastor and the prophet need to relate in a healthy local church:

1. The prophet submits to the pastor. The prophet recognizes that the pastor has the anointing of God to lead the church, and that the pastor is the final authority.

2. The prophet hears from God. This is the gifting that the prophet has. I do not mean that the pastor does not also hear from God, but look at Amos 3:7: "Surely the Lord

God does nothing, unless He reveals His secret to His servants the prophets."

3. The prophet communicates what he or she hears to the pastor. At this point maturity and discernment will guide the prophet as to how much to say, when to say it, and how to communicate the message from God graciously.

4. The pastor judges, interprets, strategizes, and executes the will of God as expressed in the prophecy. Here is where many prophets fall into a trap. They may not think that the pastor is making the right choices, so they switch into a mode that they shouldn't and try to control or intimidate the pastor. When they do this, they begin to look like the prophet on the cover of *Ministries Today.*

I wouldn't suggest that these four points embrace the total protocol for pastors to relate to prophets. But they are a good starting point for allowing a local church to prosper as God wants it to. The other chapters, written by pastors, provide much more detail.

A Pastor Who Did Not Prosper

I will conclude with the true story of a pastor who did not prosper because he did not listen to the prophets in his church. This pastor, whom I will not name, had an unusual anointing of God for his ministry. He was leading a rapidly growing megachurch. The community regarded him as a strong family man. He was highly respected by other pastors in his city and in the nation. He was in constant demand to speak at conferences and seminars. Many looked to him as a role model.

Recently, he was tempted to enter into a romantic relationship with a church member. Keep in mind that he wasn't the first. Many other pastors have likewise been tempted. However, this pastor made a decision to have an affair with her, fully understanding how dangerous it could be to his ministry and to his family and to his church. Soon after the affair began, God spoke to some prophets (intercessors) in the church. They did not know what was happening, but their message was, "Pastor, there is something going on that is not right. God says that if you will repent now, no one will ever know about it."

This was the grace and mercy of God being offered to this pastor. If he had listened to the prophets he would have prospered. But he chose to continue his affair which, after ten months, was exposed and caused irreparable damage to his family, his church, and untold numbers of other Christians. Even if he is somehow restored down the road, his ministry will never be all that God intended it to be.

None of our pastors or our churches deserves this kind of disaster. This is why it is urgent that we develop and agree on our rulebook of protocol for the relationship of pastors and prophets. The following chapters, written by seasoned pastors, will help take us a long way in the direction we need to go.

Notes

1. *Ministries Today* May/June 2000 cover property of Strang Communications. Used by permission.
2. "Letters," *Charisma*, August 1999, pp. 9-10.
3. "Y2K: A Look Back," *GI News*, Vol. 9, No. 2, June/July, 2000, p. 13.

CHAPTER THREE

PASTORING THE PROPHETIC

by Stephen L. Mansfield

Stephen Mansfield is the senior pastor at Nashville's Belmont Church who is known for his passionate teaching, strategic vision, and sense of humor. Stephen holds a doctorate in the fields of history and literature, ministers in many nations throughout the world, and has written a number of books on history and leadership, including *Never Give In: The Extraordinary Character of Winston Churchill*, and *Faithful Volunteers: The History of Religion in Tennessee*. He lives in Nashville with his wife, Patricia, and their two children, Jonathan and Elizabeth.

Perhaps you've heard this humorous bit of conventional wisdom: A pure evangelist left to himself will build a large but shallow church, the classic mile-wide-but-inch-deep-in-the-things-of-God church. A pure pastor left to himself will produce a church of people with deep relationships, but who don't have enough vision to find their way out the door. A pure apostle left to himself will produce a chaotic church because he's never there—he's always out being "translocal." A pure teacher left to himself will turn the church into a lecture hall: First Church of the Egghead. And the prophet? The pure prophet's church is usually a small group of well-beaten sheep.

We Need Each Other

Overstated perhaps, but more true than we might want to admit. The fact is that our gifts, even for leadership, were never meant to function alone. We need each other. We need the teaming of the five-fold ministry that makes the body of Christ balanced and strong.

Another way to say this is, we each have a destiny, but our destiny is fulfilled in connection with others. None of us was issued all the equipment we need to fulfill our purpose, much less reveal Jesus to a dying world. We need others around us with different tools and different skills. Truly we have an individual destiny, but that destiny is fulfilled in a corporate setting.

There are many applications we can make of this truth, but one of the most pressing for today is the connection between pastor and prophet. As God is restoring powerful prophetic ministry to the church, He is also teaching us to weave the prophetic into the corporate expression of the five-fold ministry, to tether the prophetic to the complimentary gifts that make the prophet a success. No ministry is more important to this success than that of the pastor, so let's consider some of the keys to effectively pastoring the prophetic.

The Path of the Prophet

Before we do this, let's think about who these prophetic people really are, even though we may have to generalize a bit to get a picture of them.

People called to prophetic ministry were likely born with an exceptional level of spiritual sensitivity. They may have been artistic in nature or perhaps literary, or they may have found that their visionary gifts made them leaders among their peers. Most likely they were misfits, outsiders, sensitive souls who felt the blows of the world deeply. Even if they were esteemed, they seldom experienced society as though they were part of it. They were often misunderstood by their parents and made to feel like "black sheep." Their spiritual gifts in an unredeemed state made them intensely aware of invisible realities but without mooring to the truth, so some of them veered into the occult and false mysticism. All this was simply the photographic negative of their calling, the imprint of a divine destiny on their unredeemed souls.

When these prophetically gifted people came to Jesus, they usually came with unrestrained passion. They had found, like all of us, the answer to their soul's cry. They were hungry. They fed ravenously on the Word of God and gave themselves with abandon to pure worship. Streams of truth and compassion merged in them and they were often astoundingly generous. They were usually fascinated with signs and wonders and reveled in the raw power of God.

Knowing the Mood of God

In time, they began to sense the imprint of their unique calling. They developed a keen sense of God's presence and knew when He wanted to speak to His people. They sensed His moods and His burdens of heart, even before they knew exactly what they were feeling. It was wonderful, but it also confused them because they often felt squeezed between what God wanted to do and the religious routine going on about them. Their tendency to think in terms of black and white made them impatient with compromise and gray areas. They couldn't understand why others didn't see things as clearly as they did.

It got worse. Prophetic gifting often comes with dramatic flair, with volume and tears and flamboyance. This brings criticism and charges of arrogance. Prophets, often lacking the character to sustain the weight of their anointing, make mistakes. They can be critical, impulsive, and proud. After all, pastoring and teaching are fairly common gifts, a dime a dozen. But a prophet? He or she can "read your mail," speak the dark mysteries of your soul, and unveil your "prophetic" destiny. Who needs anything else?

So the church either idolized prophetic people or suspected them, used them or rejected them. And they were messy. Not just their ministries, but their lives. The truth is that teachers can teach anything whether they have lived it or not, but prophets usually have to live what they proclaim. Their life is an object lesson in revelation and it can be a pretty shattering experience.

Keen Insight, But Blind as a Bat!

This is a picture of the prophetically gifted. Bold and insecure. Accurate and missing it by a mile. Possessing keen insight into spiritual mysteries and blind as a bat when it comes to natural realities. They can prophetically tell another individual everything they've ever done or are going to do, but they can't hear God for the simplest thing about their own lives!

The prophetically gifted are coming to your church! In fact, they may already be there!

So what do you do? You learn to pastor them. You learn what Paul taught in 2 Corinthians 10:8 and 13:10, that the authority of a Christian leader is for building people into what they are called to be and not for tearing them down. You learn that the anointing you have is a flow of grace and insight to help people with every kind of gift fulfill their divine destiny. You reclaim your calling to bring the body of Christ into maturity and you accept the truth that this won't get done without prophetic ministry. You remember that pastoring is like tending a garden: keep away the varmints, pull the weeds, feed what's growing, water well, and don't expect mature fruit overnight. And you welcome the humbling truth that you can't provide everything your church needs. You need the prophetic.

Pastoring the Prophet

There are many tasks involved in pastoring prophetic people that are also common to pastoring people of any kind. For our purposes here, though, let's just focus on two of the tasks that are of particular importance when pastoring prophets.

The first of these has to do with wounding of the heart. Given the path that most prophets have had to walk, both as Christians and before, there is usually an exceptional need for attending to issues of wounding and bitterness. If these aren't addressed, the prophet will likely gravitate to an isolated, critical, and hardened condition of heart that can quench the

prophetic fire. If these issues are addressed successfully, however, there can be a greater love and wholeness and thus a
clearer prophetic flow than ever.

Healing Bitterness

Most prophets, like most Christians, have been offended at
one time or another. In the New Testament, the word "offended" is translated from the Greek word *scandalon*. This
word was used in the ancient world to describe the part of a
trap on which the bait was set. This image helps us understand that when we are offended, we have taken the bait of a
trap that has been set for us. And who set the trap? Paul told
Timothy in 2 Timothy 2:24-26 that offended people have been
taken captive by the devil to do his will. So, traps of offense
are set for all of us by the devil who wants to dominate our
lives. One of the ways he dominates us is with the bitterness
that offense releases into our souls.

It is interesting that bitterness is presented in the Bible as
a kind of sharp, pungent poison. It's like bitter bile. This is
why avoiding offense and an offended nature are so important. These traps of offense inject the bile of bitterness into
whomever they capture and leave them tainted and defiled.

This means that bitterness defiles both the spirit of a person and the "flow" that feeds his or her gifting. Have you
ever heard someone speak true words that left you on edge
because of what you sensed coming from their spirit? This is
because when someone's spirit is tainted, everything that flows
from their spirit is tainted. Prophets are particularly suscep-
tible to this, both because of the hard path they have usually
had to walk and because the anointing on them is often so
strong. The power of the anointing can often amplify what is

in their hearts, making a bitter heart a putrefying experience for all who hear them.

Pastors must help prophets see the destructive work of bitterness in their lives. Is the prophet extremely hard edged? Is there a critical nature to his or her teaching or a judgmental attitude in the prophecies they give? Is the prophet like a wounded puppy when dealing with others, running away at the least pinprick of offense? All of these can signal a heart of bitterness, which can end up being a disqualifier for the ministry. Remember that in Acts 8:20-23, Peter told Simon that he had no part in the ministry of the Spirit because his heart was full of bitterness. Bitterness is dangerous and has to be cleansed through repentance, forgiveness, washing by the word, and the healing love of the body of Christ.

Biblical Balance

A second area for the pastor to focus on in tending the prophet is in the area of biblical balance. Prophetic gifts are often so strong and so wonderful that it is easy for the prophet to develop this single gift apart from biblical truth and doctrine. This will weaken the gift and leave the prophet open to making doctrinal errors based on revelations unchecked against the purifying truth of Scripture. Many dangerous heresies have arisen from just such a disconnect between prophecies and Scripture.

It is essential for prophets and their followers to understand that the Word and the Spirit *always* agree. To leave being biblical in order to be spiritual is serious error. The two have to be merged and the pastor must help the prophet see this need and open the prophet's life to a deepening in biblical truth and theology. If we understand that prophecy is not only *foretelling* (telling the future) but also *forthtelling* (speaking forth the truth of God) the need for this biblical balance is all the more clear.

Pastoring the Prophetic Message

Most everyone who has been around prophetic ministry has more than one horror story about prophetic words that led people into extreme actions. For some, such tales become a basis for avoiding the prophetic and blaming prophets. The truth is that the prophet usually isn't to blame. The blame rests with our immaturity in knowing how to judge prophecy. Paul tells us in 1 Thessalonians 5:19 to not treat prophecies with derision but to test them and hold onto the good. For a pastor who is welcoming prophetic ministry in the church, knowing how to judge prophecy and training others to do the same is essential to hearing the word of God and avoiding disaster.

Let's consider the example of Paul. In Acts 20:22 where Paul said that he was compelled by the Holy Spirit to go to Jerusalem. He had heard from God. He was going. But while on his journey, Paul went through Tyre and the disciples there "through the Spirit" urged Paul *not* to go (Acts 21:4). Clearly, this speaks of the gifts of the Spirit, including prophecy. Yet, Paul continued on his journey, for the next verse says, "When our time was up, we left and continued on our way."

Before long, Paul and his team ran into Agabus, who tied his hands with Paul's belt and said, "The Holy Spirit says, 'In this way the Jews of Jerusalem will bind the owner of this belt and will hand him over to the Gentiles'" (Acts 21:11, NIV). Even members of Paul's team tearfully urged him to turn back, but Paul continued. Later, in chapter 23, Jesus said that Paul's presence in Jerusalem was indeed God's will: "Take courage! As you have testified about me in Jerusalem, so you must also testify in Rome" (Acts 23:11, NIV).

Clearly, God led Paul to go to Jerusalem. Clearly Paul received two instances of prophetic input that seemed to urge him *not* to go to Jerusalem. Paul had to judge these words, to test them against what he knew. The words from the disciples in Tyre he judged to be wrong, perhaps motivated by human compassion rather than the Spirit of God. The prophetic act of Agabus, Paul had to interpret correctly. Agabus never said, "Don't go." He merely told what would happen if Paul did go. Paul interpreted the act correctly, as instruction, not dissuasion, and he went, fulfilling God's will.

Seeing through a Glass Darkly

This is such a critical teaching for us. Obviously, those who receive prophecy must know these lessons. Yet it is also important for prophets to humbly accept the truth that they see through a glass darkly, that they know only in part. In other words, they make mistakes. Mature prophets urge everyone to whom they prophesy to judge, test, and compare with Scripture everything they say. They are not offended when people are careful, when they rightly view prophecy as a call to prayer before action. Such an attitude will make for a healthier, less liable ministry, and it will evidence a level of character that will allow God to entrust the prophet with greater power and accuracy.

Pastoring the Prophetic Team

One of the most important truths for the pastor to imbed in

the heart of a prophet is that the prophet is part of an equipping team. This has two elements. First, the primary job of the prophet according to the Ephesians 4 vision is to equip the saints. Every mature prophet understands this and is eager to raise up prophets and to mature the body as much as to prophesy. But it is also important for the prophet to understand that he or she is part of an equipping team, positioned by the Lord with the other members of five-fold leadership to serve the body of Christ.

This is a critical truth for prophets. More so than those of other gifts, prophets have a tendency to be loners. This is often because of the wounding we've already discussed. As powerful as their gifts may be, they will never fulfill the calling of God and have the full impact they are called to have unless they learn to team with other leadership gifts. The wise pastor will help prophets understand this dynamic and nurture a "team-able malleability" in their souls.

Because prophetic ministry is so dramatic, there is also a tendency in the body of Christ to exalt it over other the ministries of Ephesians 4. This is a critical error for several reasons. First, each of the five-fold ministries brings needed truth and power to the church without which imbalance and weakness prevails. This we already know. But it is also true that there is a prophetic element to all of the ministries in the Ephesians 4 list. Pastoral ministry is very difficult without prophetic insight. Apostolic ministry is virtually impossible without it.

Prophets have a role in encouraging the prophetic element of all the gifts as well as receiving the imprint of those gifts on their own ministry. All this the wise pastor can nurture and encourage. It is a matter of welcoming the prophetic in its place rather than idolizing the prophetic and thus deforming the body of Christ.

A Dream Come True!

For years believers have had a dream: that powerful prophets might arise in the church. This has happened and now a greater dream is becoming reality. God is granting not just individual prophets, but a prophetic people. This is happening largely because of the ministries of wise pastors; pastors who not only welcome the prophetic, but tend it well, with a firm, loving hand and biblical truth. The work of such pastors is among the greatest reasons for hope that a truly prophetic church will arise in this generation.

You will have respect because of 2 things:
1) age + 2) education; but you will gain genuine
friendship by the love + compassion exhibited +
the joyful attitude. The barrier will be
fear re you having a superior status.

Your challenge is to be yourself as I made
+ want you to be, - a mature leader who
is humble of heart with no need to super-
-impress anybody, especially the know-it-alls.

Know that this will be a delicate place
to be in at times requiring prayful
preparation + listening to H.S. re accepting
invites to ministers. Mostly you will leave
a good impression due to their heart attitude
as true pastors and your fatherly ways.

Some, hurting + insecure pastors, with fears
before you even come, will remain unmoved
+ resistant, until My Grace shows them
your apostolic mantle (not you). Then they
will yield to the Power and submit willingly
There will be a few whom I will send you to
who need to repent, and some whom will
teach you things + really bless you ->

CHAPTER FOUR

HOW PASTORS RELATE TO PROPHETS

by Mike Bickle

Mike Bickle is director of the International House of Prayer of Kansas City, a 24-hour-a-day citywide spiritual warfare ministry. In addition to being ministry director of Friends of the Bridegroom, a ministry dedicated to equipping forerunners in the beauty of God, he is also president of the Forerunner School of Prayer, a full time training school in Kansas City. The au-

thor of two books, _Passion for Jesus_ and _Growing in the Prophetic_, Mike's teaching emphasis is in the area of developing passion for Jesus through the knowledge of the beauty of God.

One of the most significant issues in raising up the pro- phetic ministry in general is, specifically, how pastors relate to prophets.

The Whole Congregation Must Understand

The prophetic ministry in the local church functions best when both the pastors and people in the congregation have a unified view of how things should operate. In our church, Metro Christian Fellowship of Kansas City, there are many people who have had some kind of prophetic dreams, visions or impressions on a regular basis. Many have a word from the Lord that relates to the life of the church. Nevertheless, we seldom have spontaneous prophecies voiced from the congregation. Neither do we plan a routine pause for prophetic words after three good worship songs. It is important for unity and peace for the whole church to understand how the prophetic ministry functions. Therefore, the principles for nurturing and administrating prophetic ministry need to be understood not only by pastors and prophets but by the congregation as well.

Being a Pastor When You're Not a Prophet

Some people are surprised that I have pastored prophetic people without being prophetically gifted myself. I have had private conversations with many wonderful pastors who were frustrated because they were not able to move in spiritual gifts as freely as some of the people in their congregation. Often, however, some of these prophetic-type people in the church can be spiritually immature in other ways. Here is what can happen. Pastors can feel insecure, thinking that their prophetic people are apparently more "in tune with the Spirit." Consequently, they feel too intimated to correct the spiritual weaknesses in such people. This is not a good situation.

I seldom prophesy, and even when I do, there is no "thus saith the Lord" tagged on for emphasis. If I have something I feel is from the Lord, it will usually come out in my preaching and teaching without my mentioning it as a prophetic word. While some pastors feel pressure to sound more spiritual because of their leadership position, I have been careful to tone down any appearance of prophetic giftings because of my position as senior pastor of the church.

When other pastors realize that I am a pastor-teacher with very limited prophetic giftings, their response is often something like this: "I never realized you could have this kind of thing happening in your church and survive as a pastor without being a prophetic person yourself." It is very important to understand that it doesn't take a prophet to nurture and administrate prophetic ministries in your church. It takes a leader with a vision for a multi-gifted, diverse team.

All the Gifts Are Needed

Pastors and teachers serve a different purpose than prophets and evangelists who have predominantly power gift ministries. God wants all the gifts to rest in a body of people not just in one or two leaders. One person functioning as both the head prophet and the senior pastor can present a conflict of interest similar to what would have existed in the Old Testament if a single individual were to hold the office of both high priest and king. I'm not at all saying it is unbiblical to be both the strongest prophetically gifted person and the senior pastor. I am saying it is rare, and when it does happen, it involves a set of added pressures that normal pastors do not face.

There is a fresh wind of the Holy Spirit blowing all across

the world today. With each new outpouring of the Spirit come unusual and unexpected manifestations. For example, the disciples appeared to be "drunk" on the day of Pentecost. This current moving of the Spirit is only a beginning of a spiritual deluge prophesied in the end times. The church desperately needs wise and mature pastors-teachers who can lead, nurture, and administrate their prophetic people in the midst of such a supernatural outpouring.

All of us, including pastors and prophets, need to learn to be secure in what God has called us to be and to realize the value and importance of each person. Paul, in his letter to the Ephesians, was explaining the different gifts and callings in the church when he wrote: "The whole body, being fitted and held together by that which every joint supplies, according to the proper working of each individual part, causes the growth of the body for the building up of itself in love" (Eph. 4:16 NASB).

Satan Sows Discontent

Satan wants to prevent this from happening. He is a master of sowing discontent into people's hearts about who they are and what God has called them to do. This is a problem throughout the whole body of Christ. People are always leaning over the fence, longing for the other cow's grass. I have met numerous prophetic people who want to be teachers. They clearly see all the pain associated with their prophetic gift, and they imagine that the teacher has only success, respect and a life of appreciation. Many teachers that I know who have seen genuine prophetic people say that they want to prophesy. This can add up to a dysfunctional church. We all should be happy to be what God has decided we should be.

One of my main callings is in the area of intercession. For years I have found grace to cry out for a revival of passionate Christianity across our nation. I was content within those limited spiritual boundaries before I had ever heard of any contemporary prophetic people. That became a real key for me when God's time came for me to relate pastorally to some strong prophets.

Prophets Can Intimidate

One of the most important lessons I had to learn was that I did not have to be intimidated by people who heard directly from God much more frequently and much more dramatically than I did. It was not easy. At first I was terribly reluctant. Here I was, a pastor in my late twenties relating to strong prophetic ministers who regularly received profound and accurate prophetic words. At first, my tendency was to be intimidated. My consequent reluctance to confront prophetic people when they needed it came to a head around two years after the prophetic ministry started in our church.

This was 1984. For some time I had been sitting by and watching five or six strongly prophetic people regularly compete for the microphone during the Sunday morning services. I was starting to get exasperated because it was becoming clear to me that there was a lot of hype in what had been going on for the last few months. Some members of the congregation were getting tired of feeling manipulated by these prophets and they were starting to voice their feelings.

"Dueling Prophets Sunday" ✓

I'll never forget one Sunday morning in December 1984 when

two of our main prophets got into a "prophetic duel" right in front of the church. One stood up and proclaimed something to this effect: "Thus says the Lord, 'A great thing is going to happen.'" Then the second guy stood up and said, "Thus says the Lord, 'Better things are going to happen.'" Then the first one took the microphone and topped him. Not to be out-prophesied, the second prophet answered back by giving something even better. They went about three rounds each!

I sat on the front row getting really angry. It was clear to me what was going on. These two guys were yielding to a common fleshly temptation among prophetic people and were competing against each other for the position of the top prophet of the church. It was scandalous, embarrassing, and ridiculous. Everybody in the church could see it except these two prophetic men. A dozen people came up to me afterwards and asked me how much longer I was going to let this go on. Previously I had tried to cover for the prophets by encouraging people to be patient, reminding them of all the great things that had happened. But this time they had gone far over the line. Like the legendary emperor, these prophets had no clothes, and the only ones who didn't know it were these two prophetic men themselves.

I realized that if I was the pastor of the whole church, I had to pastor these two prophets as well. So I got both of them together and we had what turned out to be a very strong and direct confrontation. Both of them were defensive. They threatened that if I didn't accept their ministry style and what they had to say, the Holy Spirit's blessing would leave our church. I was really surprised they would resort to such fleshly means of manipulation because previously they had given prophetic words about the future that had already come to pass exactly as they had predicted. But when they issued this ultimatum, it pushed a button in me. My eyes opened, and, at that point, I saw the rank carnality in all of it.

"I'm Finished with You Guys!"

Up to that time, I would have been intimidated by people who had previously prophesied with such astounding accuracy. But I was provoked and offended, so I rose up and told them both to leave the church. I essentially informed them, "I'm finished with you guys!" That was such a disillusioning time for me that I was tempted to get rid of all the prophetic ministry, the miracles, the supernatural confirmations—everything, and we would no longer have prophetic ministry in our church. I was about to revert to peaceful, traditional religion!

I'm glad now that I didn't give in to my anger and frustration because of the marvelous things that I've seen God do in our church through the prophetic ministry since then. But there was one very positive thing that came out of what we now call "Dueling Prophets Sunday." Something broke inside of me and from that point on, I was no longer afraid to confront prophetic ministers, even if they had previously had authority to call fire down from heaven.

What Offended Prophets Can Do

Both of the prophetic ministers told me that they were finished with this church, and they assured me that God was canceling all the tremendous prophetic words spoken over the church. They assumed that God was going to leave with them. It sounds silly to me now, but there was a time that I would have thought that God's blessing might really leave if these prophets got their feelings hurt and left. But God doesn't abandon you just because a prophetic minister gets offended. The

Holy Spirit can use prophets mightily and effectively, but they are not the mediators between God and us. Only Jesus is.

Surprisingly, these two offended prophets began to complain against me to some of the key people in the church. But these church members called me up and congratulated me saying, "Thank you, thank you, Pastor, thank you!" That's when it began to dawn on me that it was not the prophets who had the gifting and calling of governmental leadership in our local church. I also realized that if we leaders don't stand up and speak the pastoral wisdom that God has given us, the prophetic people could not only destroy the church, they could destroy their own ministries as well.

Much of what happened on "Dueling Prophets Sunday" was my fault because I had not exercised my pastoral leadership gift and responsibility. I had allowed these men to get themselves into a difficult and embarrassing situation. I realized that the team of governmentally gifted people in our church had a lot more pastoral wisdom than the prophets did about church life and how people respond to the Word of God. In one short week, the way I viewed my own ministry and that of our pastoral leadership team totally changed.

A Happy Ending

Within two weeks both of those prophetic men came back and repented to me of their ambition and carnal motivations. This put a new confidence in me that some of those deep uneasy feelings that I had about their ministry style was really pastoral wisdom and discernment. I determined that I was no longer going to dismiss or quench those feelings again. Since that encounter, I decided that whenever I get a nervous feeling about what the prophetic people were doing, I would not ignore it. To neglect the pastoral responsibility to lead the prophets and correct them when necessary will usually result in harm to the church and to the prophetic ministers themselves.

Shell-Shocked Prophets

Many prophetic people get in touch with their giftings long before they cultivate the corresponding wisdom, humility and character that is necessary to succeed in prophetic ministry. In the beginning, they may appear arrogant or pushy because of their zeal. As years go by, their pushiness usually increases because of fear, hurt, and rejection. Most prophetic people who have been around for a few years have had their hands slapped many times. Some of them have been dealt with harshly, without proper explanation and without the security of a good relationship with church leadership.

By the time I met most of prophets who joined our church they had been mistreated by many people and they had deep ministry scars. In other words, they were shell-shocked by negative experiences with previous churches. The average person who has been in the prophetic ministry for 10 years is pretty beat up and bruised. This is especially true if the prophetic gift was active in their early years. By the time they are 40 or 50 they are often very guarded and suspicious of authority figures. Those coming in to prophetic ministry later in life may also have problems with rejection. Past histories of dysfunctional relationships with leaders in the church can cause prophetically gifted people to overcompensate by seeking honor and acceptance. Many problems can develop if prophets give in to those temptations.

A Hunger for Credibility

Some prophets are attempting to build up enough credibility to insure that they won't be rejected. Many of them just want some security. Everyone knows you don't cut a great athlete from your basketball team just because he may have one bad game. Since building clout is so important to many prophets, there is the temptation to push hard to get credit for having accurately heard from God. I personally do not think it is always appropriate to publicly acknowledge the person who gave me a key prophetic word as I share it with the church. However, a rejected prophet can hardly resist letting others know, "Oh, I'm the one who gave him that key prophecy!"

Sometimes prophetic people come into conflict with pastors because they push too hard for their revelations to be spoken at the public church services. If the pastor doesn't give the prophetic minister a public platform in the church, a temptation for the prophet is to judge the pastor as having a controlling spirit. Sometimes people with this attitude will go so far as to gather their prophetic groupies together to pray against the pastor.

All of this (and more) is usually a result of wounded and rejected prophets giving in to former hurts and present temptations. The problem is also amplified by pastoral leadership that does not see beyond the prophetic person's pushiness in order to discern the inner fears and hurts that drive them. If prophetic people, who are misunderstood, wounded and rejected, give in to their fears and temptations, they may tend to go overboard in their efforts to obtain credibility and acceptance. But, ironically, it will inevitably backfire on them. The harder they try, the worse it gets. The unfortunate fact is many of them have not yet figured this out.

Why Pastors Won't Confront Prophets

Pastors are usually reluctant to confront a seasoned prophet. Why? Because they have their own insecurities. In my case, I was very much aware of my inability to hear from God like the prophets did. I therefore operated on the premise that if the prophets could receive such divine information, certainly they could also hear from God on how to apply it. I soon learned that I had made a false assumption.

Knowing where and how to draw the line with prophetic ministry minimizes the insecurity and fear that a pastor normally experiences when first encountering such people. If pastors understand how to deal with these people, they are less afraid of them. Most pastors don't mind if things are a little messy if it is going to be profitable at the end of the day. But if they don't see the long-term benefit, they're going to say, "Enough of this!" and press the reject button. For the most part, pastors don't want to be embarrassed, and they don't want their people becoming hurt and confused. They are trying to protect their people and keep peace in the church.

Prophets usually have a very keen sense of being answerable to God. Pastors have that sense too, but they are also very aware of being answerable to people. A pastor probably feels both concerns differently from the typical prophet. Pastors realize they are answerable to God but they also know that if there is a problem, on Monday morning they are going to hear about it from the elders and from half of the congregation.

Many pastors yield to insecurity and the fear of what others might think of them. They've seen too many churches fail and so many people hurt by it. They sometimes get their eyes off God and shy away from anything beyond the comfort zone. They must avoid this. Pastors of healthy churches must learn to lead without fear, but also without sacrificing pastoral wisdom.

Stretching Boundaries

Most pastors I know are willing to let unusual, unprogrammed, and even some strange looking things happen as long as they are convinced that it is not hype or fake. However, pastors are often sensitive to things happening beyond what is of the Holy Spirit. They would rather be safe by cutting things off a little before getting into the danger zone. Their boundaries tend to be on the conservative side.

On the other hand, prophets tend to be boundary stretchers. They are almost always willing to go a little bit farther than the danger zone to make sure that we do everything that might be of the Lord. If we do a little bit too much, in their way of thinking, it's better than not doing all of it. The biggest fear of prophets is that they might not get everything unloaded that God wants unloaded. The biggest fear of pastors is that they don't want to get the church into hype because they have to maintain a long-term relationship with the people.

Notice that both prophets and pastors have the same motivation. They are afraid of missing God. But they each are proceeding from different points of view.

A Gifted Team Makes a Healthy Church

The church's greatest effectiveness is realized when the diversity of gifts and personalities work together as one team ministry. But it takes a lot of patience and honoring of one another to deal with the pressures that come with nurturing and leading a church with a variety of giftings. Unless we learn to show honor to each other and the unique work that the Holy Spirit is doing in each person's life, we may wind up in a holy war, especially if the gifts and personalities are strong. Without team ministry, none of these gifts would be able to prosper. But with God-directed team ministry we will have healthy churches.

CHAPTER FIVE

THE TRUE PROPHET
IN THE LOCAL CHURCH

by Kingsley A. Fletcher

A crowned king of the Shai state from the West African nation of Ghana, Dr. Kingsley Fletcher is an internationally acclaimed inspirational and motivational speaker, philanthropist, government advisor, and author of eight books, including *Prayer and Fasting, I Have Seen the Kingdom* and *The Power of Covenant.* Dr. Fletcher serves as senior pastor of Life Community Church in Research Triangle Park, North Carolina, where he resides with his wife, Martha, and their daughters Anna-Kissel and Damaris Joy.

Contrary to what is commonly thought, not all believers are in hot pursuit of a "Word." Many, in fact, shudder at the very thought of being in the presence of a prophet. This mentality is not scriptural. Although believers are to honor the office of a prophet, they are also responsible to validate the ministry of prophets rather than fear what they speak. 1 Corinthians 14:29 instructs us in this manner: "Let two or three prophets speak, and let the others judge" (NIV).

To appreciate and support the ministry of prophets, the local church must first understand how important that ministry is for the church to be healthy. Secondly, the church must be able to discern who is a "true" prophet in order to validate or refute his or her ministry. This chapter will address these two points of reference.

Prophets: One of the First Gifts to the Church

Prophets were one of the first gifts given to the church as seen in two very important Scriptures:

1. "And God has appointed these in the church: first apostles, second prophets, third teachers…" (1 Cor. 12:28 NIV)

2. "It was he who gave some to be apostles, some to be prophets, some to be evangelists, and some to be pastors and teachers, to prepare God's people for works of service, so that the body of Christ may be built up until we all reach unity in the faith and in the knowledge of the Son of God and become mature, attaining to the whole measure of the fullness of Christ" (Eph. 4:11-13 NIV).

As noted in these Scriptures, prophets play a key role in the life of the local church. They are responsible to declare the word of the Lord. Their declarations bring direction and clarity for the purpose of establishing the body of Christ.

The words of a prophet should always be constructive. There-fore, the pastor must carefully scrutinize anyone addressing the congregation as a prophet since the prophetic office serves to impart, direct, and inspire the people. False or negatively spoken words can leave lasting impressions that hinder rather than advance the vision and the purpose of God for the local church.

It is imperative that the authenticity of a given prophetic ministry be tested at its very outset in a local church. Aspects which should be tested include personal spirituality, submission to authority, personality traits (i.e., selfishness, glory seeking), the nature of prophecies given, and whether they come to pass. Careful consideration of these aspects is vital when a professed prophet is in the house!

Prayer and Fasting

All the attributes that distinguish a true prophet are important, but first and foremost is the prophet's great willingness and obedience to the Lord. True prophets live a consecrated life, one of prayer and fasting so that they can hear the voice of God and obey accordingly. A keen ear is necessary to discern the spiritual climate in a church and the issues currently being faced. Prayer with fasting causes prophets to be perceptive to the direction in which God would have the church to proceed. How can prophets declare a "word," unless they have heard a "word" from God? What level of accuracy can their ministry entail, if they are not sensitive to the leading of the Holy Spirit? It is only through an awareness of God, fellowship with Him, and prayer that the true prophetic anointing is developed.

The Lord Jesus Christ, the greatest of all prophets, is the best example we can follow in the area of prayer and fasting:

"Jesus full of the Holy Spirit, returned from the Jordan, and was led by the Spirit into the desert, where for forty days he was tempted by the devil. He ate nothing during those days, and at the end of them he was hungry" (Luke 4:1-2 NIV).

It was prayer and fasting that established the authenticity of Jesus' prophetic ministry. Yes, He operated in the gift of prophecy, but His role as a prophet went beyond the gift. His consistent ability to discern a matter and then accurately address it was based upon His intimate relationship with the Father. This type of relationship was the result of prayer and fasting. If Jesus, the prophet who spoke the greatest of truths, prayed and fasted, how can a prophet of today be "true" unless he or she follows His example?

Submitting to the Authority
of the Pastor

Prophets truly called of God outwardly submit to the authority of the pastor in the church where they are ministering. They are conscious of the principle of pastoral authority and they always defer to the "set man" of the house. As one of the five-fold ministers, prophets completely understand church government and the role they play. Genuine prophets never try to take over, control or elevate themselves above the pastor. Instead, they publicly affirm the shepherd to the flock.

They are mindful to convey that the prophetic ministry is *supplemental* to and supportive of what is already being taught in the church and never to be seen as a replacement, much less a contradiction. Prophets will avidly cooperate with the vision of the church, referencing facets of the vision during their time of ministry. Their total support of the pastor and submission to the apostle (where one is present) is evident in the words which true prophets speak.

Scripture confirms that prophets, regardless of their level of anointing, are expected to submit their ministry to designated authority. This is seen in 1 Corinthians 14:32: "The spirits of prophets are subject to the control of prophets. For God is not a God of disorder but of peace" (NIV). If prophets are properly in control of the message they bring, they most certainly can comply with the wishes of a host ministry. To do otherwise, would be a blatant act of disobedience and a red flag to the congregation that such a person is not a true prophet!

The Message Aligns with Scripture

It should go without saying that a prophet's message must align with Scripture. Anything spoken contrary to God's law is to be rejected. This is referenced in the Old Testament: "If a prophet, or one who foretells by dreams, appears among you and announces to you a miraculous sign or wonder, and if the sign or wonder of which he spoke takes place, and he says 'Let us follow other gods' (gods you have not known) 'and let us worship them,' you must not listen to the words of that prophet or dreamer" (Deuteronomy 13:1-3 NIV).

Although signs and wonders many times accompany a prophet's ministry, they should never distract people from the truth. The most important element is the spoken word for it commands either life or death. There was severe punishment imposed in the Old Testament when false prophecies were given. Prophets were put to death. This is a stern reminder of what happens when lies are allowed to replace truth.

Do the Prophecies Come to Pass?

Another means by which to judge the authenticity of prophets is whether their predictions come to pass. If a prophet's predictions do not come to fruition then his or her prophecies should be tabled or put on hold. Notice that I have chosen the word "tabled" rather than "rejected." Believers should be cautious not to reject a prophecy or the prophet too quickly. Although prophets are gifted in declaring the word of the Lord, they do not know everything about every person or situation.

For example, we must be mindful that there is a timing and season for a prophetic word. Therefore, it is quite possible that a true word can be spoken before the appropriate time. This may occur when a prophet is immature and their ministry not yet fully developed. Consequently, time must be allowed for the manifestation of the prophecy. It is good to remember that God speaks through a human being—a willing, yet imperfect, instrument. We should then allow for grace.

When to Reject Prophecy

There are, however, five instances when given prophets and their forthcoming prophecies should be absolutely rejected rather than tabled. These instances include:

1. They are in heresy.

2. They obviously have impure motives.

(3.) They are not called, but self-appointed.

4. They are arrogant and rebellious.

5. They are divisive.

Prophecy Is Conditional

When judging prophecy, we are to also remember that any prophetic word is *conditional*. We as believers must ensure that our life aligns with the conditions specific to the prophecy. Suppose, for instance, that you receive a prophecy stating you will become a millionaire. Conditions specific to this prophecy would include you being a good steward of money and faithfully tithing. If you don't meet these conditions, you can't expect to be a millionaire! God won't go against the principles He has established in Scripture regarding money or any other area of our lives in order for a prophecy to be fulfilled.

Examining the type of message that prophets bring further tests their authenticity. The purpose of prophecy is to edify, exhort, and comfort. Hence, true prophets will bring words of edification to the local church, not destructive speech. They will seek to build up the church body into the structure that God wants it to be. The words of the prophet will pour the oil of gladness on areas of roughness within the church, bringing a soothing and comforting admonition to the people of God.

True Prophets Edify

The message of true prophets is edifying. It is not judgmental or suspicious. Rather, they are sensitive to the people's weaknesses, not wanting to expose believers, but to help them. Although they are very direct in speaking truth, genuine prophets love people and they are long suffering. They reveal God's word only to redeem. Prophets, however, are expected to declare divine judgment when gross sin and evil are present and there appears to be no indication of repentance.

Prophecy attracts many people in search of inspiration. Therefore, it is most important not to disillusion them with harsh words. God cannot trust someone as a prophet whose nature is insensitive, impatient, unloving, and critical. He trusts only those who can see the goodness in people and those who always see the mercy of God. A kind heart is indeed characteristic of a true prophet.

Watch Out for Self-Representation!

Self-representation has no place in the prophetic ministry. Prophets always speak to the people of God in the name of the Lord. They are wise enough to know that all revelation comes from God and anything spoken apart from the anointing leans toward error. Just as the Holy Spirit does not speak of Himself as noted in John 16:13, "He will not speak of his own; he will speak only what he hears." (NIV), neither does a true prophet.

The lives of true prophets are centered on abiding in the vine (John 15:4), because they are very much aware of their inadequacies. They realize that they are incapable of bringing forth even the smallest of utterances without the direction of the Lord. Even Jesus spoke of His dependency upon His Father in John 5:30 when saying, "By myself I can do nothing; I judge only as I hear, and my judgment is just, for I seek not to please myself, but him who sent me" (NIV).

Men and women who stand in the office of a prophet are very cognizant of the fact that they are merely vessels who have been selected to speak the heart of God to the people. They realize the grace and kindness that has been afforded them, knowing it is a privilege and not a right to operate in the prophetic. True prophets make certain that God receives all the glory, never drawing attention to themselves. The prophet Jeremiah knew wholeheartedly the source from where his messages came as referenced in Jeremiah 1:9, "Then the Lord reached out his hand and touched my mouth and said to me, 'Now, I have put my words in your mouth'" (NIV).

True Prophets Are Generous

Prophets ordained by God are never self-serving, but they believe in giving to others. They are generous towards God and people. The gift of generosity and hospitality accompany their ministry. It would be difficult for God to trust someone with revelation who is stingy or greedy or who mismanages money. Therefore, a local church and its pastor should beware of anyone who prophesies for personal gain.

Unfortunately, sometimes those with the gift of prophecy appoint themselves as prophets in order to use the gift to prey on gullible people, attaching a monetary figure to the words they speak. True prophets will not desire anything materially from those to whom they minister. They will not prophesy to get something out of you. If prophets have a material need, they will be direct with you and express the need as Elijah did to the widow at Zarephath as noted in the following passage of Scripture:

"Elijah said to her, 'Don't be afraid. Go home and do as you have said. But first make a small cake of bread for me from what you have and bring it to me, and then make something for yourself and your son. For this is what the Lord, the God of Israel, says: 'The jar of flour will not be used up and the jug of oil will not run dry until the day the Lord gives rain on the land.'' She went away and did as Elijah told her. So there was food every day for Elijah and for the woman and for her family. For the jar of flour was not used up and the jug of oil did not run dry, in keeping with the word of the Lord spoken by Elijah" (1 Kings 17: 13-16 NIV).

Elijah could not have been any more direct with the widow regarding his need. Case in point: true prophets leave nothing to speculation, as their speech is precise and sometimes very blunt. Prophets of integrity do not concern themselves with what people think and they are willing to die for what they speak. Therefore, they do not have to employ gimmicks such as "selling prophecies." They are most comfortable in sharing whatever need there might be with believers in the local church, but always with the permission of the pastor.

Prophets Speak Blessings

If you notice, Elijah not only made his need known to the widow, but he also spoke a blessing upon her. Prophets having a sincere heart will speak blessings upon the people and stand in agreement with them until the blessing comes to pass. They will not receive anything from the people without taking into consideration the needs of the people as well.

In conclusion, a true prophet can be a tremendous asset to the local church if God's divine attributes are evident in their lives. Their ministry can help in taking the church to another level in experiencing the power of God. They can make the difference between a sick church and a healthy church. However, if this is to happen, we as believers must be willing to assume our responsibility as it relates to validating and supporting this office of prophetic ministry given for the perfecting of the saints.

Here is a golden opportunity, already "built in" by Me, for one another. There are many things to consider beforehand [ie re the "launch"] in order for relationships to solidify.

1. The Kingdom must be first, and it's "growth"
2. "   "   "   mindset must prevail over any Church or ministry!
3. Love of Me & eachother must guide all actions

This does not mean that there will not be any differences or viewpoints that won't be a challenge. Cultures of age, nationalities, times & seasons, bkgds, schooling will all still be there to sort out & blend.

However, if you go back and look at My first Words you can note 3 phrases: "golden opportunity" & "built in" & "by Me for each." Study & chew on them! Then, watch, yes, watch & see what I will do re much on the part of Me for you both, and for The Kingdom! Amen!

CHAPTER SIX

THE SPIRIT OF WISDOM
AND REVELATION

by Tom S. Hamon

Tom Hamon and his wife, Jane, are Senior
Pastors and Apostolic Overseers of Chris-
tian International Family Church in Santa
Rosa Beach, Florida. They travel world-
wide training and activating leaders in
their spiritual gifts. Tom also serves on the
Board of Governors and is a Regional Ap-
ostolic Overseer in Christian International
Network of Churches under Bishop Bill

Hamon. He has an Associate's degree from Christ for the
Nations Institute and a Bachelor of Theology from LIFE Bible
College. Tom and Jane reside with their three children in
Santa Rosa Beach, Florida.

Having had the privilege of pastoring a prophetic church
in Santa Rosa Beach, Florida, Christian International
Family Church, for the past 14 years, I have seen a lot of things

that I know were truly prophetic and some that were definitely pathetic. If there is any ministry in the body of Christ that needs training, truly it is the prophetic ministry. It is one of the most powerful tools for good and blessing in the body, but one of the most potentially dangerous in the church at the same time.

Like the knife in the hand of the unruly that can so easily cut or maim, the same knife in the hand of a surgeon can operate and heal. So the prophetic has the great potential for building or destroying depending on the skill, training, equipping, and intent of the one using the instrument. I believe that is why the sons of the prophets were being diligently mentored and trained by Samuel and Elijah in the Old Testament (1 Sam. 19:20; 2 Kings 2).

Pastors Must Embrace the Prophetic

I have found that if pastors do not choose to embrace the prophetic, then they will have a weak and only partially equipped church for the true vision God has released for His body. Their church will not be as healthy as God desires. At the same time, if you don't diligently train people in proper prophetic protocol and principles, and purpose to consistently exhibit the real and genuine, then either you will feel compelled to essentially shut the prophetic down in an effort to maintain order, or you will open the door for the flaky, the weird, and the counterfeit. It's funny that when the real is being powerfully manifested the false seems so impotent.

The joint ministries of pastor and prophet have the opportunity to form the dynamic duo of the New Testament. However, this relationship is also one that has been fraught with turmoil throughout church history. I believe the main reason for this has been a lack of appreciation on both parts valuing each other. The Apostle Paul goes to great lengths in the Scriptures to create an atmosphere of appreciation for the diverse parts and giftings which God has given as different expressions of His nature within His body. The difficulty enters relationally when we don't value a certain part of the body that God Himself has given. We usually don't value something because we don't understand its purpose or positioning and thus, what we don't understand we have the tendency to ignore or abuse. The more understanding we have the more opportunity we have for dynamic working relationships.

Pastors and Prophets

In Ephesians 1:17, the Apostle Paul prays a prayer for the Ephesian Christians to come into an understanding of their true calling, inheritance, authority and power. In the initiation of this prayer the Apostle talks about two dynamics of the Spirit which he feels these Christians must receive in order to truly grasp their destiny. He prays that the Lord "may give unto you the spirit of **wisdom** and **revelation** in the knowledge of Him" (KJV, bold added).

I believe that the pastoral office correlates more to the spirit of *wisdom* and the prophetic ministry more exemplifies the spirit of *revelation*. Often times there is a perception gulf that grows between the prophet and the pastor. Because of the gift of revelation, a prophet may have the tendency to see things very black and white, whereas a pastor, with mercy and wisdom, will often see things in shades of gray.

How does this play out? The prophet many times may view the pastor as compromising and people pleasing while the pastor may see the prophet as unwise and unyielding. These differences in perception can become a deficit to their working relationship, if not understood as strengths that God has given to aid one another in being more effective in ministry. Otherwise, the prophet will always try to straighten out the pastor and the pastor will always strive to balance out the prophet, when more often their differences, when appreciated, are actually their strengths.

A Desire for Wisdom

In Ephesians 1:17 we see that revelation is most effectively ministered in the context of wisdom. Many times the biggest challenge for prophets is not necessarily in hearing the voice of God, but in learning how to minister the word in wisdom. This speaks of the timing, the manner, the place, the wording, the intent, the context, and the attitude of heart when ministering.

When prophets are truly operating in the spirit of Christ, their overarching desire is not to be heard or to be vindicated as accurate but rather to be a blessing to help build the church by strengthening the hands of the leaders and edifying those they minister to.

James says that the spirit of wisdom has to do with meekness and humility which destroys the very foundation for strife in the church (see James 3:13). The prophetic ministry must constantly guard itself against the spirit of pride which would cause a prophet to usurp a place of authority in the local church over the head of that church by claiming divine inspiration.

Avoiding Criticism
and Rebellion

A prophetic word or discernment should never be thrown in the pastor's face as vindication for a critical spirit or rebellion. Any type of corrective word for leadership should not be given publicly but should be submitted in a private setting very prayerfully, respectfully, and full of the spirit of humility. Too many lone ranger, independent prophets acting as sheriffs in the body of Christ have left a bad taste in the mouths of pastors because of the intimidation that can come by one saying, "Thus saith the Lord..." with personal agendas in mind.

The prophets as part of the five-fold ministry team in Ephesians 4:11 are called to help build and equip the church, not to tear it down. Prophets are not called to be independent operators but they are called to be part of the team and they must learn to submit to godly authority as much, or even more, than anyone else.

Part of the problem associated with prophets arises because they often see things that others don't. And they usually see them long before they come to pass. This can be a frustrating position to be in. That's why Scripture says to take My servants the prophets who have spoken in the name of the Lord as examples of suffering, affliction and patience (see James 5:10). This means that prophets will have to be especially careful not to get a persecution/rejection complex because of the suffering that often accompanies the call. And patience must be prized as a virtue worthy of our purposeful efforts to attain, otherwise the ungodly tendency to become disgruntled and frustrated, and thus a problem instead of a blessing, looms before us.

Prophets Need
to Feel Understood

Often these difficulties are amplified when a prophet does not feel understood or valued for the giftings God has given him or her or the call upon their life. If there is no proper and sanctioned place or position for true prophets to operate in the local church, they often will begin to seemingly work in a subversive way in an effort to release the ministry God has given them.

I am not saying that this is right, however, it is many times the case because no recognition, protocol, or place of release has been given for the true operation of prophetic ministry within the church. This is clearly the responsibility of the pastor. The pastor is the only one who is positioned to rightly raise up, authorize and release prophetic ministry in the local church.

In turning our attention to the pastors in this process, let's ask ourselves this question: Why do so many pastors ignore or totally subdue prophetic ministry in their churches, even though this is expressly addressed in Scripture? Scripture says of prophetic ministry: "Quench not the Spirit, despise not prophesying" (1 Thess. 5:19,20 KJV); "Let the prophets speak...let the other judge" (1 Cor. 14:29 KJV); "He gave some...prophets...to equip the saints for the work of the ministry, for building up the body of Christ" (Eph. 4:11 KJV); "...touch not my anointed and do my prophets no harm" (Ps. 105:15 KJV); The Lord said, "I will send them prophets and apostles, some they will kill, some they will persecute" (Luke 11:49 KJV).

Jesus went on to say that the religious leaders of that day had taken away the key of knowledge, and He was going to hold it to their account that they wouldn't enter in and those that were entering in they hindered. Yet why do many pastors still reject the prophets today?

Why Pastors Can Be Antagonistic to Prophets

There are many reasons for an attitude of indifference or even antagonism toward prophetic ministry by pastors. Some reasons have to do with ignorance concerning the need or purpose of prophetic ministry, or with perceived abuses of those who have called themselves prophets within the body. However, I do not believe these are valid excuses today.

Never in Scripture does God sanction forbidding the true and good because there have been bad representations. In fact, God was very displeased with Israel because they rejected Samuel's prophetic leadership and asked for a king because Samuel's sons had apparently abused their positions. God very clearly said to Samuel "they have not rejected you but they have rejected me" (1 Sam. 8:1-8).

As pastors, many times prophetic ministry can understandably make us feel uncomfortable, so we don't give place for it to function. However, often that is exactly what God has intended because we have become stuck in a rut in our predictable, comfortable routines. There are times when God wants to break in on the scene, but we are too protective of our time or our people or our comfort zones to allow God to really do what He wants. Prophets just seem to have a way of messing up our plans as they see in the spirit. Instead of resenting this, fellow pastors, let's appreciate it, because the good news is that when God leads prophets they bring a powerful spirit of breakthrough with them.

Praise God, He is releasing more and more mature demon-
strations of prophetic ministry as well as more teaching and
understanding about the proper place and function of prophetic ministry in the church. It is more imperative than ever
for pastors to be attuned to what God is doing in the church
today and thus to be prepared to equip and release their people
in their God-given gifts and callings.

Pastors also may tend to be intimidated by the prophetic
because they don't feel proficient in this area of ministry themselves. Just as prophets need to purpose to develop the
wisdom of how to rightly minister their revelation, so pastors need to stretch themselves to believe to minister by
supernatural revelation and not just rely upon their developed areas of wisdom and counsel.

Sometimes pastors can even have a tendency to become
jealous of the dynamic anointing and charisma that often accompanies an accurate prophet's ministry. However, the
more secure we are about God's ability to speak to us and
through us, the less opportunity there will be for us to feel
threatened by prophetic ministry. Some pastors would just
prefer not to be bothered with the potential messes created
by having the word of the Lord released among the people in
their church. However, this is not a satisfactory position for
leaders to take once they understand the vital role prophetic
ministry can play in releasing the destiny of individuals and
the church. Churches can survive without prophetic ministry, but they cannot be as healthy as they should without it.

Dealing with False Words

I can honestly say that over the 14 years of overseeing both personal and public prophetic ministry in our local church, there have only been a handful of false or harmful words which we've had to deal with. Most of the time it's a matter of training people to operate in their gifts with more wisdom and maturity. However, I have received thousands of testimonies on how the word of the Lord has changed someone's life, breathing new life into them and putting them back on a path toward God's purposes and destiny.

Granted, it takes time and effort to incorporate prophets and prophetic ministry into the leadership team and life of the local church, but the benefits are substantial and well worth the effort. Let me just take a moment and touch on some practical points for positive relationships between pastors and prophets.

Prophets:
Be Loyal and Submissive!

Prophets, if you are not the head of the local church, you must demonstrate your unwavering loyalty and commitment to the success of the leader (pastor) of the church. Your position is a place of support, using your gifts to build the church. When a pastor sees that evidenced in your ministry, he or she most likely will relax, receive from you, and release you to fulfill your calling. If this doesn't happen, then God will take care of you like he did David with Saul, if you can keep your heart right like David did.

Let me also say to prophets, don't be afraid to submit your revelation to your pastor and allow him or her to use the gift of wisdom and position of authority to decide how, when or if to implement the thrust of your word. Give what you have and leave it with the pastor. It then becomes the pastor's responsibility before the Lord, not yours. Don't become critical or judgmental if the pastor does not move as fast or in the way you expect. Be faithful to do your part and allow them to do theirs.

It is always important to operate in the open under the blessing of your local church leadership so that no one needs to doubt what you are doing or where you are coming from. In Christian International, we require that all prophetic ministry be tape recorded in order to maintain clear accountability with the leadership of the church concerning what is being ministered. Prophets, be careful not to disconnect or isolate yourself from your pastoral leadership. Constantly, consistently, openly, and wisely communicate. This is both for your protection and your blessing.

Pastors:
We Don't Know It All!

Pastors, it is a fallacy to believe that we must have it all or know it all concerning our position of leading our local fellowship. God has purposed to make us reliant upon one another as well as upon Him. Prophets have a key of revelation that will help unlock places of hindrance and bring breakthrough in times of need. Many times we can form mindsets about how things are or how they ought to be. What a blessing it is to have someone attuned to the voice of the Lord to help us to see past a blind spot in our lives and ministries and help us get God's perspective again. That's what Nathan did for David. That's what Elisha did for his servant. And that's what a prophet can do for a pastor when they value each other and know they are out for each other's good.

Wisdom and revelation are a <u>powerful team</u> that helps bring health to the church when the pastor and the prophet are <u>working together</u> and not fighting each other! I believe that is <u>what God intended</u> to help bring His church into its finest hour!

<u>Part II</u>

Tues Oct 1, 2013 @ 11:30 am   WoL to/for JH & JM re this

You've waited a long time to see growth locally, especially for the ministry in this region. Must you be reminded that "much prayer availeth much"? Well, I've heard you and all those prayers over the many years, and "now let the weak say that they are strong ... because of all that the Lord have done for thee" as a good God & Father!

And now, slowly, an opportunity is opening up and will continue to do if handled correctly My Way! Yes, he's from a different orientation the Faith movement, just as you are from a combined " " of the Charismatic - Power Evangelism - Messianic type of org. Jachel is, like you, open with a heart on fire for Me

Note that his focus is on young unchurched adults, just the target your last public prophecy thru Bob Jenkins in Newtown 5 yrs. ago, said. Well I'll see how I can move in My Time + Manner (Way)?

Remember, there are distinctions between local church & specialized ministry, although they can work together and even be blended with great harmony, with one being an outgrowth of the other. Usually an accurate ministry spawns a local church from home groups. Other times it is the " " that spawns other ministries. In this case, as with some others, the two come alongside each other and blend for awhile until I bring about new changes to accommodate new directions to accomplish My purposes.

For now, explore & cooperate mutually and I will show "the Way" (Mine) knowing that you are each separate entities functioning together for a common purpose The Kingdom! If you agree to do this without any hidden agendas for self or org' you represent, I will bless both your respective joint effort & yourselfs, because you then are obeying Me, thus showing your love for Me & each other. HS will guide you through any bumps in this journey. Know that this will be a joy & fun, because I AM this Way and want you both to experience this in your relationships

SUBJECT INDEX

New Covenant, 13-14
New York Times, 27
Newsweek, 27
Nineveh, 27
Noah, 27

O
occult, 35
Old Covenant, 13-14

P
Passion for Jesus, 45
pastoral wisdom, 52, 56, 73
pastors, authority of, 28-29, 62-63, 74, 79
pastors, intimidation of, 25, 46-47, 49, 51, 75, 78
pastors, office of, 9-11
Paul, 40-41, 48, 73
Paul-Silas relationships, 19-20
Peter, 39
Pierce, Chuck, 20
prayer, 61
Prayer and Fasting, 59
prophecy and Scripture, 39-40, 63-64
prophecy of warning, 28
prophecy, conditional, 65
prophecy, definition of gift, 14
prophecy, divisive, 65
prophecy, edifying, 65-66
prophecy, false, 78-79
prophecy, judging, 40-41, 63-65
prophecy, rejection of, 64-65
prophetic gifts, 39
prophetic people, 35-37, 46, 48, 50, 52, 53
prophets and apostles, 19-20, 63
prophets and evangelists, 18-19
prophets and intercessors, 18

prophets and teachers, 18
prophets, antagonism toward, 77
prophets, confrontation of, 51-52, 54-55
prophets, office of, 9-12, 60, 67
prophets, rejection of, 53-54, 77
Protestant Reformation, 9
protocol for pastors and prophets, 29-30
protocol, prophetic 16, 17-31, 72
Psalm 105:15, 76

R
rebellion, 75
Roman Empire, 7

S
Samuel, 72, 77
1 Samuel 8:1-8, 77
1 Samuel 19:20, 72
Satan, 48-49
Saul, 79
scandalon, 38
spirit of pride, 74
spirit of revelation, 71-81
spirit of wisdom, 71-81
spiritual gifts, 48
Surprised by the Power of the Spirit, 15
Surprised by the Voice of God, 15

T
teachers, 14, 15, 17, 18, 34, 48
teachers, office of, 9-11

WAGNER

LEADERSHIP INSTITUTE

Founded by Dr. C. Peter Wagner, Wagner Leadership Institute (WLI) trains and equips men and women for leadership in local churches and other ministries.

This radical new approach to education emphasizes practical ministry experience, anointing, and impartation. Because practical training and impartation are the goals of each course, no grades are given for courses, events, or training experiences taken for credit. Nor are there exams. Rather, field research, apprenticeship, mentoring, and ministry experience are deemed as valuable as library research or classroom attendance. Our goal is to equip leaders with the necessary skills for effective ministry. Entrance requirements are not based on academics, but on age, ministry experience, and maturity.

WLI provides an earned training credential for church and ministry leaders who desire ordination, licensing, or other forms of public recognition by awarding diplomas for Associate of Practical Ministry, Bachelor of Practical Ministry, Master of Practical Ministry, and Doctor of Practical Ministry.

For more information on Wagner Leadership Institute visit our website at:

www.wagnerleadership.org

or call us at:

1-800-683-9630

Apostles of the City

How to Mobilize Territorial Apostles for City Transformation

C. Peter Wagner

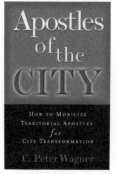

In recent years the Body of Christ has seen some important principles for city transformation set in place. While there have been many short-term successes, city after city reports that their efforts over the long haul are not producing the city transformation that they have worked so hard to accomplish.

So, what are we missing? How can we see our cities become all that God intended them to be? This book examines how recognizing and affirming apostles of the city might well be the most vital missing link for seeing our cities truly transformed!

Discover the answers to many questions, including:

- What strategic changes need to be made in my city in order to see it truly transformed?

- Who is an "apostle of the city," and how are they set in place?

- What are the three crucial concepts I need to know that will lay the proper groundwork for city transformation?

- Is my city prepared for the moving of the Holy Spirit that will bring real transformation in the near future?

This important new book is for everyone who wants to see their city move beyond short-term successes into the genuine transformation that God desires to bring!

Leadership
Paperback • 58p
ISBN 1.58502.006.0 • $6.00

Hard-Core Idolatry
Facing the Facts

C. Peter Wagner

This hard-hitting book will help clear away many questions about idolatry and how it has permeated churches today. Readers of this book will:

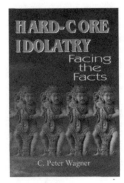

- Understand the difference between hard-core and soft-core idolatry

- Feel the pain of God's broken heart when His people worship idols

- Recognize idolatry, even in some of our churches

- Be able to confront Satan's schemes with more understanding and power

- Begin to cleanse their own homes of ungodly objects

Christian Living/Spiritual Warfare
Paperback • 43p
ISBN 0.9667481.4.X • $6.00

The Queen's Domain
Advancing God's Kingdom in the 40/70 Window
C. Peter Wagner, Editor

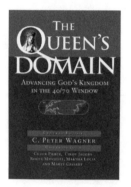

Does prayer really change the world? Without question the answer is yes! This book will encourage any Christian by showing dramatic answers to prayer that has radically changed the world in the 1990s and has put us in the midst of the greatest spiritual harvest the world has ever known. So, where do we go from here?

In *The Queen's Domain*, C. Peter Wagner has pulled together five top Christian leaders and intercessors who show where the Body of Christ is headed in prayer in the new millennium for an even greater harvest! Together they answer many questions including:

- Who is the "Queen" and where is her domain?

- Why are there so many unsaved "Christians" in the 40/70 Window?

- How will fervent prayer for the 40/70 Window have a ripple effect throughout the world?

- How can we transfer wealth from the Queen's Domain into the kingdom of God?

- How is prayer for the 40/70 Window different from prayer for the 10/40 Window?

Spiritual Warfare/Prayer/Missions
Paperback • 127p
ISBN 1.58502.009.5 • $8.00

Confronting the Queen of Heaven

C. Peter Wagner

This book takes a look at what is perhaps one of the most powerful spirits in Satan's hierarchy: the Queen of Heaven. Throughout history this high-ranking principality has kept countless multitudes of lost souls blinded to the gospel.

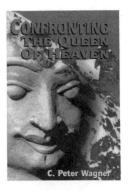

In this book, C. Peter Wagner takes a look at how the Queen of Heaven has accomplished her goals in the past, and how she is manifesting in the world today to keep untold numbers in spiritual darkness. This book will help you discover how God is mounting an assault against this dark force to see the captives set free!

Spiritual Warfare/Missions
Paperback • 42p
ISBN 0.9667481.3.1 • $6.00

Available at finer bookstores
or by calling toll-free 888-563-5150

Revival!
It Can Transform Your City

C. Peter Wagner

This book takes you beyond city taking to city transformation!

Questions addressed include:

- What exactly is revival?

- Can a city actually be transformed through revival?

- How can Christians move to new levels of spiritual warfare to see revival come?

- What new wineskins is the Holy Spirit using to facilitate revival?

- What steps can be taken to sustain revival in a city?

Discover how the Spirit of God can visibly transform cities through the revival we have been praying for.

Leadership/Spiritual Warfare
Paperback • 63p
ISBN 0.9667481.8.2 • $6.00

Radical Holiness For Radical Living

C. Peter Wagner

Holiness has long been a topic
of great debate. In this easy-to-
read book, C. Peter Wagner
helps bring clarity to the topic
by answering many questions
including:

- Can anyone really live a
  holy life?

- Is there a test of holiness?

- What are the non-negotiable principles for
  radical holiness?

- How much holiness should be required of a
  leader?

For any believer who wants to be everything God
wants them to be, this book will open the way for
them to move to new levels in their Christian
lives. Through radical holiness, readers will learn
to defeat Satan's schemes and enjoy daily victory
in their walk with God!

Christian Living
Paperback • 41p
ISBN 0.9667481.1.5 • $6.00

Seven Power Principles

That I Didn't Learn in Seminary

C. Peter Wagner

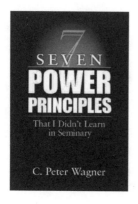

God is moving with power in the world today! In this book, Wagner captures 7 key principles for moving in that power.

"God is alive and active today but the evidence of His activity is often difficult to find in Evangelical seminaries and the churches pastored by seminary graduates. Peter Wagner is a standard-bearer for the growing numbers of Christian leaders and churches that are moving with God beyond the drag of intellectualism. This book is a worthy summary of what God has been teaching many of us since seminary. I pray that God will use it to point the way for many more church leaders to follow the Holy Spirit's guidance beyond what they learned in seminary."

Dr. Charles Kraft
Professor of Anthropology and Intercultural Communication
Fuller Theological Seminary, Pasadena, California

Leadership/Spiritual Warfare
Paperback • 86p
ISBN 1-58502-014-1 • $7.00

Mon 10/7/13 WoL to JH (a JD) ee matters

It's not easy for a young "pastor" to be "#1" in a new "territory." Many factors enter in, especially being a "light-weight" compared to a "heavy" like you (punt). Be careful of "overwhelming", like K.

Let not silence, absence of contact, etc concern you all. Pray and let things be for awhile.

Fri 11/15   contact gently